Fancy Fringed Ornaments

by Jamie Cloud Eakin

Published by JCE Publishing
Copyright © 2008 Jamie Cloud Eakin
All rights reserved.
ISBN-10: 0692307699
ISBN-13: 978-0692307694

Table of Contents:

Intro:

There is nothing like the luxurious beauty of fringe! I love to wear it **and** look at it. These ornaments celebrate not only the fabulous nature of the beads, but the wonderful look of fringe.

One Christmas, I gave many of these ornaments as gifts. To my pleasant surprise, they were never packed up after Christmas, but were hung on stands, hooks, on shelves in windows, etc. When asked, the gift recipient replied "they are too wonderful to see for such as short time of year at Christmas only". I took their advice too, and use them as an interesting home décor item.

The ornaments in this book work on a basic design and vary from there using different colors and bead sizes. The purpose of this is to allow you to make different ornaments, but still get faster with each one. As you make these designs, you'll see your comfort level and speed increase with each additional ornament. This is important since everyone you know will want one!   Another added benefit is you'll find this is a wonderful way to get the confidence to make your own design.

Fringed Ornament – Fire Flowers

Supplies:

7 grams sz 11 seed beads red transparent AB

14 grams sz 11 seed beads orange transparent AB

3 grams sz 11 seed beads yellow transparent AB

2 grams 6mm bugle beads twisted dark orange AB

56 ea 4mm round beads yellow transparent

42 ea 4mm Czech Fire polish beads orange transparent

98 ea 4mm Czech Fire polish beads red transparent

42 ea 6mm round beads red transparent

42 ea 5mm bicone beads red transparent

42 ea 8mm flower beads yellow transparent

42 ea 7x10mm leaf beads orange transparent

Beading thread size A Silamide or B Nymo white

Beading needle size 12

Glass ball ornament 2 ¾ diameter

Steps:

Make a strip that will go around the glass ball:

1. Cut 4 yards of thread and put a needle on one end to work single thread.
2. Use the "Half-thread Method" so add a Stop Bead with a 2 yard tail. (Stop Bead see page 61) (Half Thread Method see page 62).
3. Pick up one seed orange, one bugle and one seed orange. Move down to the stop bead.
4. Pick up one seed orange, one bugle and one seed orange. Stitch through the previous column, then through the current column.

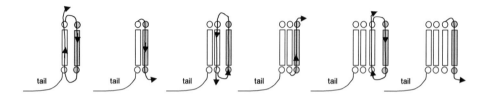

5. Repeat step 4 until there are 4 columns with bugles.
6. Pick up one seed red, one 4mm red, one seed red, one seed orange, one bugle, one seed orange, one seed red, one 4mm red and one seed red.
7. Stitch through the previous column, through the seed-4mm seed, and the current column.

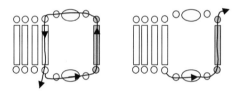

8. Repeat step 4 through 7, ending with step 5 until there is approximately 9 to 12 inches of thread left. Leave this thread end.
9. Remove the stop bead and add a needle to this tail end of the thread.
10. Repeat steps 4 through 7, starting at step 6. Stop when there are 13 sections of 4mm windows, ending with step 5. See illustration.

11. Stitch back through the strip, **all the way to the other end** to reinforce. Use the two threads and tie a square knot. Weave the ends in and cut.

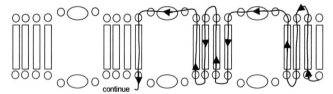

Add fringe to the strip:

12. Cut 3 yards of thread and put a needle on to work single thread. You will need to add a new thread, so if you would prefer to work with a shorter thread, feel free to do so. See page 63 for instructions on adding new thread.
13. Add a Stop Bead with a 6 inch tail.

14. Stitch up through the end column on the strip (for right handers, the left-most end, for left-handers, do the right-most end). Pick up one seed orange and down through the next column.

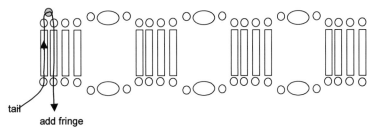

15. Create the fringe according to the Fringe Chart (at the end of the steps) until you get to the final column on the opposite end from where you started.

16. Close the strip into a circle: Pick up one seed red, one 4mm red, and one seed red. Stitch up through the column on the starting end. Pick up one seed red, one 4mm red and one seed red and stitch down through the current column.

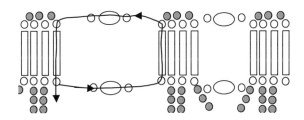

17. Repeat the thread path again to reinforce.
18. Create the final fringe.
19. Remove the stop bead, Use the tail and needle threads to tie a square knot. Weave in the ends and cut.

Create the top section (see Fitting the Ball page 63):

20. Cut 4 yards of thread and move the needle to the middle to work double thread.
21. Create a loop that will fit over the glass ball top. Use fourteen 4mm yellow beads and use enough yellow seeds to make the loop fit over the glass ball top. Pick up the beads and stitch through them again, then pull to create a loop. Tie a square knot. Leave the tail threads (used later for another knot).

   pick up: 4mm,seed,4mm,seed,4mm,seed,4mm,4mm,seed,4mm,seed,4mm,seed,4mm, 4mm, seed,
   4mm, seed, 4mm, 4mm, seed, 4mm, seed, 4mm

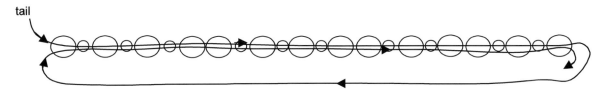

22. Pick up three seeds yellow, one 4mm yellow, five seeds orange, one 4mm orange, one 4mm red, six seeds red. Stitch through the seed-4mm-seed section on the fringed strip. Pick up six seeds red, one 4mm red, one 4mm orange, and five seeds orange. Stitch up through the first 4mm added. Pick up three seeds yellow and stitch through the 4mm in the top loop over to and through the next 4mm on the top loop.

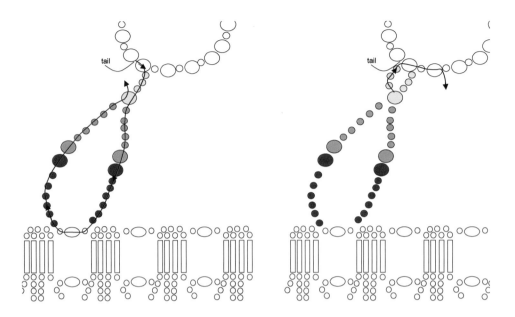

23. Pick up three seeds yellow, one 4mm yellow, five seeds orange, one 4mm orange, one 4mm red, and six seeds red. Stitch through the seed-4mm-seed on the fringed strip below. Pick up six seeds red and stitch through the two 4mm beads on the previous section.

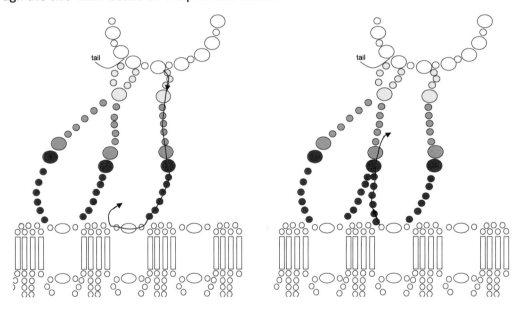

24. Pick up five seeds orange and stitch through the first added 4mm on this section. Pick up three seeds yellow and through the 4mm in the loop above and over to and through the next 4mm on the top loop.

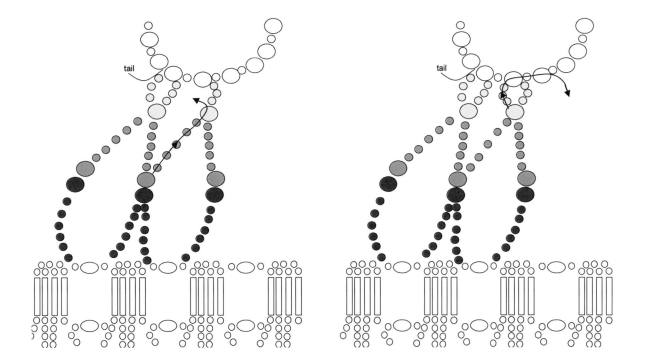

25. Repeat steps 23 and 24 until you are on the last 4mm in the top loop.

26. Pick up three seeds yellow, one 4mm yellow and five seeds orange. Stitch through the two 4mm beads in the first added section. Pick up six seeds red and stitch through the seed-4mm-seed on the fringed strip below. Pick up 6 seeds red and stitch through the two 4mm beads in the previous section.

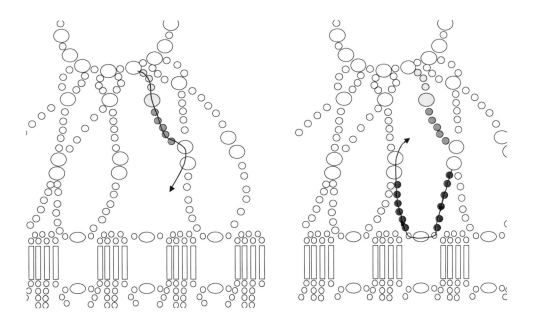

27. Pick up 5 seeds orange and stitch up through the 4mm added previously. Pick up three seeds yellow and stitch through the 4mm above on the loop over to the tail thread.

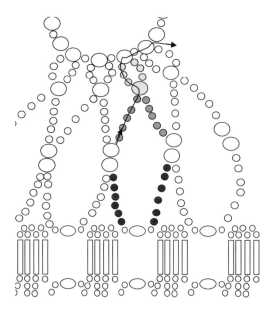

28. Use the tail threads and needle thread and tie a square knot.
29. Weave the ends in by stitching through the top loop with the needle threads in one direction and the tail threads in the opposite direction. Pull tightly and maneuver so the knot is pulled inside the 4mm bead. Cut the threads.
30. Cut 1 yard of thread and put a needle on to work single thread.
31. Add a stop bead with a 6 inch tail.
32. Stitch up through one seed above the 4mm on the top section and down through the seed next to it.
33. Pick up three seeds orange, one 4mm orange, one 4mm red and one seed red (turn bead). Stitch back through the added 4mm beads and hold the turn bead and pull to adjust the tension. Pick up three seeds orange and stitch up through the seed on top of the 4mm in the next section. Stitch down through the seed next to it.

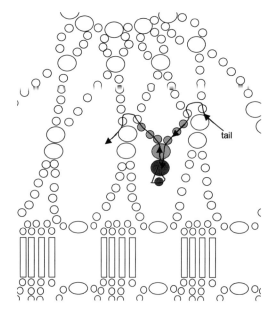

34. Repeat step 33 to return to the start.
35. Remove the stop bead. Use the tail thread and needle thread and tie a square knot. Weave the ends in and cut.
36. Done!

Fringe Chart:

Fringe: Add fringe beads, skip turn bead and stitch back up through the fringe beads plus the seed-bugle-seed above.
Hold the turn bead with one hand and thread with other hand. Pull to adjust the tension.
Pick up one seed and go down through the next column for the next fringe.

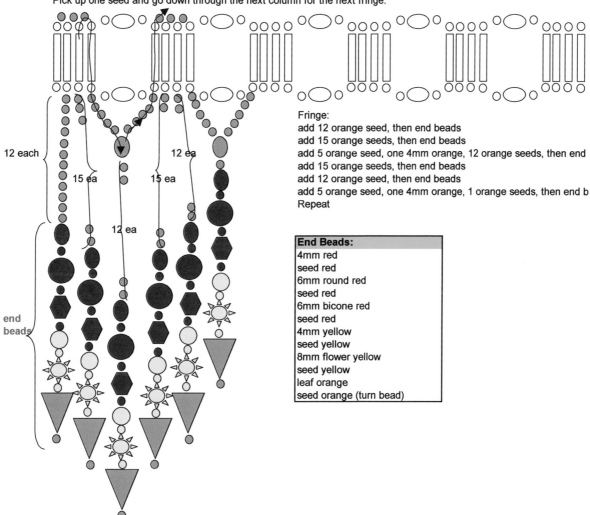

12 each

15 ea   12 ea   15 ea

12 ea

end
beads

Fringe:
add 12 orange seed, then end beads
add 15 orange seeds, then end beads
add 5 orange seed, one 4mm orange, 12 orange seeds, then end
add 15 orange seeds, then end beads
add 12 orange seed, then end beads
add 5 orange seed, one 4mm orange, 1 orange seeds, then end b
Repeat

End Beads:
4mm red
seed red
6mm round red
seed red
6mm bicone red
seed red
4mm yellow
seed yellow
8mm flower yellow
seed yellow
leaf orange
seed orange (turn bead)

Fringed Ornament – Tropical Blues

Supplies:

18 grams sz 11 seed beads turquoise AB

8 grams sz 11 seed beads teal transparent

2 grams 7mm bugle beads satin Capri blue

70 ea 4mm Czech Fire polish Capri blue

56 ea 4mm Czech Fire polish light aqua

42 ea 4mm round beads light aqua transparent

42 ea 14x4.5mm tube beads light aqua transparent

42 ea 6mm round beads teal transparent

42 ea 6mm Czech Fire polish beads blue/teal

42 ea 8mm Czech Fire polish beads dark aqua

Beading thread size A Silamide or B Nymo light blue

Beading needle size 12

Glass ball ornament 2 ¾ diameter

Steps:

Make a strip that will go around the glass ball:

1. Cut 4 yards of thread and put a needle on one end to work single thread.
2. Use the "Half-thread Method" so add a Stop Bead with a 2 yard tail. (Stop Bead see page 61) (Half Thread Method see page 62).
3. Pick up one seed turquoise, one bugle and one seed turquoise. Move down to the stop bead.
4. Pick up one seed turquoise, one bugle and one seed turquoise. Stitch through the previous column, then through the current column.

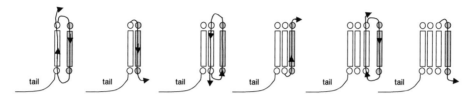

5. Repeat step 4 until there are 4 columns with bugles.
6. Pick up one seed jade, one 4mm jade, one seed jade, one seed turquoise, one bugle, one seed turquoise, one seed jade, one 4mm jade and one seed jade.
7. Stitch through the previous column, through the seed-4mm seed, and the current column.
8. Repeat step 4 through 7, ending with step 5 until there is approximately 9 to 12 inches of thread left. Leave this thread end.

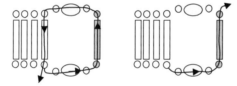

9. Remove the stop bead and add a needle to this tail end of the thread.
10. Repeat steps 4 through 7, starting at step 6. Stop when there are 13 sections of 4mm windows, ending with step 5. See illustration.

11. Stitch back through the strip, **all the way to the other end** to reinforce. Use the two threads and tie a square knot. Weave the ends in and cut.

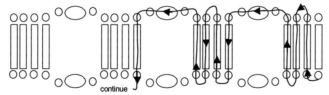

Add fringe to the strip:

12. Cut 3 yards of thread and put a needle on to work single thread. You will need to add a new thread, so if you would prefer to work with a shorter thread, feel free to do so. See page 63 for instructions on adding new thread.
13. Add a Stop Bead with a 6 inch tail.

14. Stitch up through the end column on the strip (for right handers, the left-most end, for left-handers, do the right-most end). Pick up one seed turquoise and down through the next column.

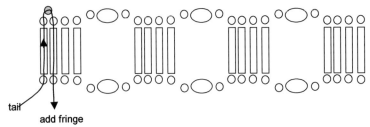

15. Create the fringe according to the Fringe Chart (at the end of the steps) until you get to the final column on the opposite end from where you started.

16. Close the strip into a circle: Pick up one seed jade, one 4mm jade, and one seed jade. Stitch up through the column on the starting end. Pick up one seed jade, one 4mm jade and one seed jade and stitch down through the current column.

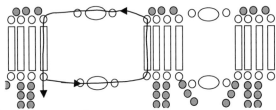

17. Repeat the thread path again to reinforce.

18. Create the final fringe.

19. Remove the stop bead. Use the tail and needle threads to tie a square knot. Weave in the ends and cut.

Create the top section (see Fitting the Ball page 63):

20. Cut 4 yards of thread and move the needle to the middle to work double thread.

21. Create a loop that will fit over the glass ball top. Use fourteen 4mm turquoise beads and use enough turquoise seeds to make the loop fit over the glass ball top. Pick up the beads and stitch through them again, then pull to create a loop. Tie a square knot. Leave the tail threads (used later for another knot).

pick up: 4mm,seed,4mm,seed,4mm,seed,4mm,4mm,seed,4mm,seed,4mm,seed,4mm, 4mm, seed, 4mm, seed, 4mm, 4mm, seed, 4mm, seed, 4mm

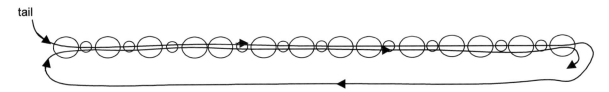

22. Pick up three seeds turquoise, one 4mm turquoise, five seeds jade, one 4mm jade, one 4mm turquoise, six seeds turquoise. Stitch through the seed-4mm-seed section on the fringed strip. Pick up six seeds turquoise, one 4mm turquoise, one 4mm jade, and five seeds jade. Stitch up through the first 4mm added. Pick up three seeds turquoise and stitch through the 4mm in the top loop over to and through the next 4mm on the top loop.

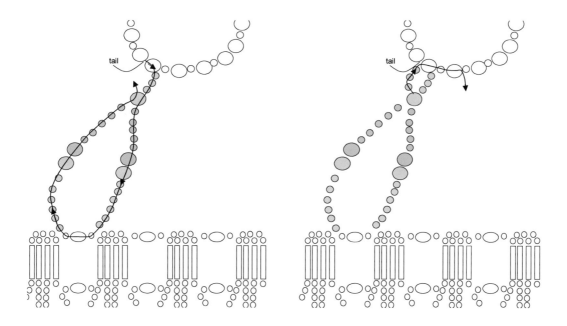

23. Pick up three seeds turquoise, one 4mm turquoise, five seeds jade, one 4mm jade, one 4mm turquoise, and six seeds turquoise. Stitch through the seed-4mm-seed on the fringed strip below. Pick up six seeds turquoise and stitch through the two 4mm beads on the previous section.

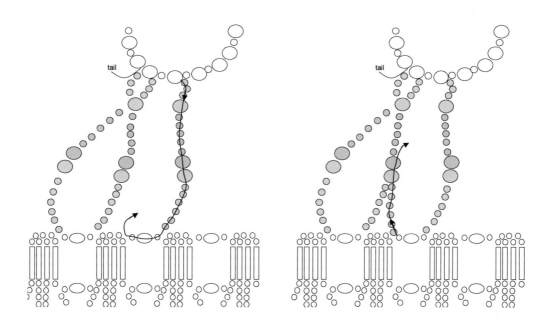

24. Pick up five seeds jade and stitch through the first added 4mm on this section. Pick up three seeds turquoise and through the 4mm in the loop above and over to and through the next 4mm on the top loop.

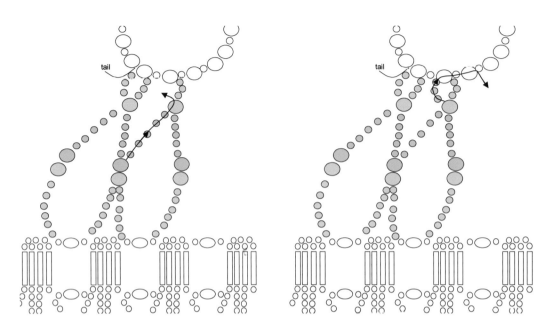

25. Repeat steps 23 and 24 until you are on the last 4mm in the top loop.
26. Pick up three seeds turquoise, one 4mm turquoise and five seeds jade. Stitch through the two 4mm beads in the first added section. Pick up six seeds turquoise and stitch through the seed-4mm-seed on the fringed strip below. Pick up 6 seeds turquoise and stitch through the two 4mm beads in the previous section.

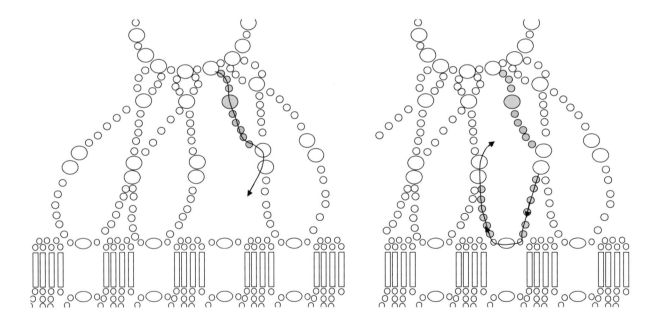

27. Pick up 5 seeds jade and stitch up through the 4mm added previously. Pick up three seeds turquoise and stitch through the 4mm above on the loop over to the tail thread.

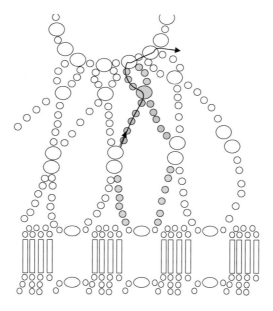

28. Use the tail threads and needle thread and tie a square knot.
29. Weave the ends in by stitching through the top loop with the needle threads in one direction and the tail threads in the opposite direction. Pull tightly and maneuver so the knot is pulled inside the 4mm bead. Cut the threads.
30. Cut 1 yard of thread and put a needle on to work single thread.
31. Add a stop bead with a 6 inch tail.
32. Stitch up through one seed above the 4mm on the top section and down through the seed next to it.
33. Pick up three seeds jade, one 4mm jade, one 4mm turquoise and one seed turquoise (turn bead). Stitch back through the added 4mm beads and hold the turn bead and pull to adjust the tension. Pick up three seeds jade and stitch up through the seed on top of the 4mm in the next section. Stitch down through the seed next to it.

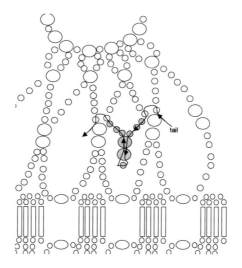

34. Repeat step 33 to return to the start.

35. Remove the stop bead. Use the tail thread and needle thread and tie a square knot. Weave the ends in and cut.

36. Done!

Fringe Chart:

Fringe: Add fringe beads, skip turn bead and stitch back up through the fringe beads plus the seed-bugle-seed above. Hold the turn bead with one hand and thread with other hand. Pull to adjust the tension.
Pick up one seed and go down through the next column for the next fringe.

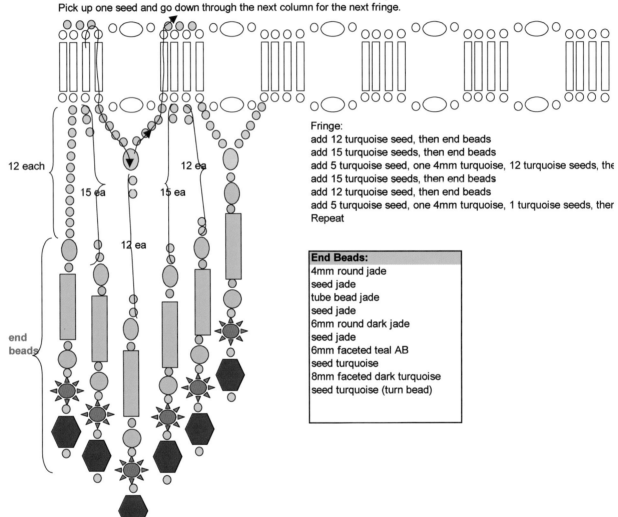

Fringe:
add 12 turquoise seed, then end beads
add 15 turquoise seeds, then end beads
add 5 turquoise seed, one 4mm turquoise, 12 turquoise seeds, the
add 15 turquoise seeds, then end beads
add 12 turquoise seed, then end beads
add 5 turquoise seed, one 4mm turquoise, 1 turquoise seeds, ther
Repeat

End Beads:
4mm round jade
seed jade
tube bead jade
seed jade
6mm round dark jade
seed jade
6mm faceted teal AB
seed turquoise
8mm faceted dark turquoise
seed turquoise (turn bead)

Fringed Ornament – Snow Pearl

Supplies:

25 grams sz 11 seed beads clear AB

2 grams 6mm bugle beads twisted clear AB

84 ea 4mm Czech Fire polished beads clear

84 ea 4mm pearl beads

42 ea 5mm bicone beads clear

42 ea 6mm round beads clear

42 ea 7x6mm oval clear crackle glass beads

42 ea 6mm pearl beads

42 ea 7-8mm round clear crackle glass beads

Beading thread size A Silamide or B Nymo white

Beading needle size 12

Glass ball ornament 2 ¾ diameter

Steps:

Make a strip that will go around the glass ball:

1. Cut 4 yards of thread and put a needle on one end to work single thread.
2. Use the "Half-thread Method" so add a Stop Bead with a 2 yard tail. (Stop Bead see page 61) (Half Thread Method see page 62).
3. Pick up one seed bead, one bugle and one seed bead. Move down to the stop bead.
4. Pick up one seed bead, one bugle and one seed bead. Stitch through the previous column, then through the current column.

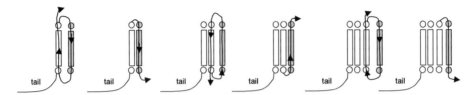

5. Repeat step 4 until there are 4 columns with bugles.
6. Pick up one seed bead, one 4mm clear, one seed bead, one seed bead, one bugle, one seed bead, one seed bead, one 4mm clear and one seed bead.
7. Stitch through the previous column, through the seed-4mm seed, and the current column.

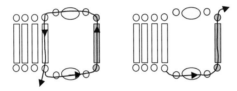

8. Repeat step 4 through 7, ending with step 5 until there is approximately 9 to 12 inches of thread left. Leave this thread end.
9. Remove the stop bead and add a needle to this tail end of the thread.
10. Repeat steps 4 through 7, starting at step 6. Stop when there are 13 sections of 4mm windows, ending with step 5. See illustration.

11. Stitch back through the strip, **all the way to the other end** to reinforce. Use the two threads and tie a square knot. Weave the ends in and cut.

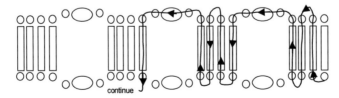

Add fringe to the strip:

12. Cut 3 yards of thread and put a needle on to work single thread. You will need to add a new thread, so if you would prefer to work with a shorter thread, feel free to do so. See page 63 for instructions on adding new thread.

13. Add a Stop Bead with a 6 inch tail.
14. Stitch up through the end column on the strip (for right handers, the left-most end, for left-handers, do the right-most end). Pick up one seed bead and down through the next column.

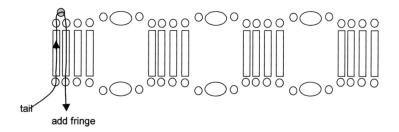

tail
add fringe

15. Create the fringe according to the Fringe Chart (at the end of the steps) until you get to the final column on the opposite end from where you started.
16. Close the strip into a circle: Pick up one seed bead, one 4mm clear, and one seed bead. Stitch up through the column on the starting end. Pick up one seed bead, one 4mm clear and one seed bead and stitch down through the current column.

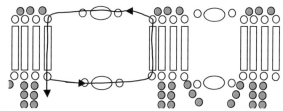

17. Repeat the thread path again to reinforce.
18. Create the final fringe.
19. Remove the stop bead. Use the tail and needle threads to tie a square knot. Weave in the ends and cut.

Create the top section (see Fitting the Ball page 63):
20. Cut 4 yards of thread and move the needle to the middle to work double thread.
21. Create a loop that will fit over the glass ball top. Use fourteen 4mm clear beads and use enough seed beads to make the loop fit over the glass ball top. Pick up the beads and stitch through them again, then pull to create a loop. Tie a square knot. Leave the tail threads (used later for another knot).

pick up: 4mm,seed,4mm,seed,4mm,seed,4mm,4mm,seed,4mm,seed,4mm,seed,4mm, 4mm, seed, 4mm, seed, 4mm, 4mm, seed, 4mm, seed, 4mm

tail

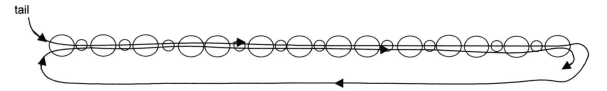

22. Pick up three seeds, one 4mm clear, five seeds, one 4mm clear, one 4mm pearl, and six seed beads. Stitch through the seed-4mm-seed section on the fringed strip. Pick up six seeds, one 4mm pearl, one 4mm clear, and five seed beads. Stitch up through the first 4mm added. Pick up three seeds and stitch through the 4mm in the top loop over to and through the next 4mm on the top loop.

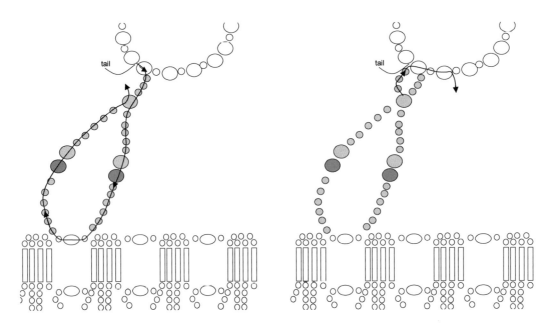

23. Pick up three seeds, one 4mm clear, five seeds, one 4mm clear, one 4mm pearl, and six seed beads. Stitch through the seed-4mm-seed on the fringed strip below. Pick up six seeds and stitch through the two 4mm beads on the previous section.

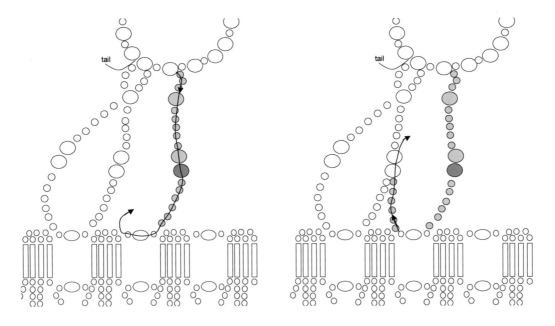

24. Pick up five seed beads and stitch through the first added 4mm on this section. Pick up three seed beads and through the 4mm in the loop above and over to and through the next 4mm on the top loop.

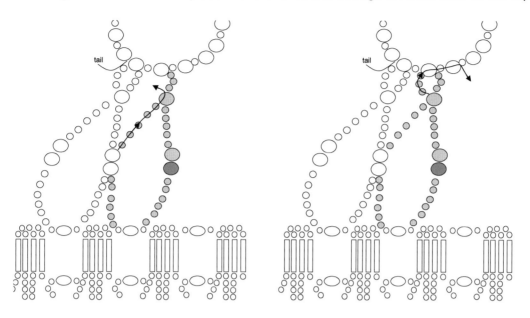

25. Repeat steps 23 and 24 until you are on the last 4mm in the top loop.
26. Pick up three seeds, one 4mm clear and five seeds. Stitch through the two 4mm beads in the first added section. Pick up six seed and stitch through the seed-4mm-seed on the fringed strip below. Pick up 6 seed beads and stitch through the two 4mm beads in the previous section.

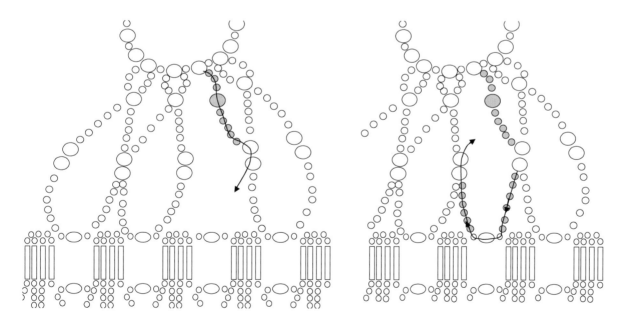

27. Pick up 5 seed beads and stitch up through the 4mm added previously. Pick up three seeds and stitch through the 4mm above on the loop over to the tail thread.

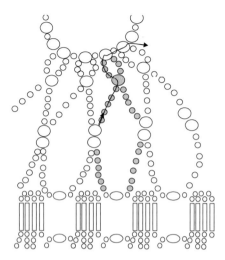

28. Use the tail threads and needle thread and tie a square knot.
29. Weave the ends in by stitching through the top loop with the needle threads in one direction and the tail threads in the opposite direction. Pull tightly and maneuver so the knot is pulled inside the 4mm bead. Cut the threads.
30. Cut 1 yard of thread and put a needle on to work single thread.
31. Add a stop bead with a 6 inch tail.
32. Stitch up through one seed above the 4mm on the top section and down through the seed next to it.
33. Pick up three seeds, one 4mm clear, one 4mm pearl and one seed bead (turn bead). Stitch back through the added 4mm beads and hold the turn bead and pull to adjust the tension. Pick up three seeds and stitch up through the seed on top of the 4mm in the next section. Stitch down through the seed next to it.

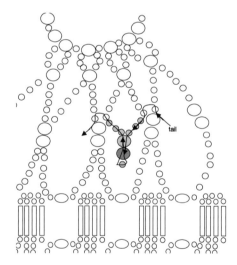

34. Repeat step 33 to return to the start.
35. Remove the stop bead. Use the tail thread and needle thread and tie a square knot. Weave the ends in and cut.
36. Done!

Fringe Chart:

Fringe: Add fringe beads, skip turn bead and stitch back up through the fringe beads plus the seed-bugle-seed above.
Hold the turn bead with one hand and thread with other hand. Pull to adjust the tension.
Pick up one seed and go down through the next column for the next fringe.

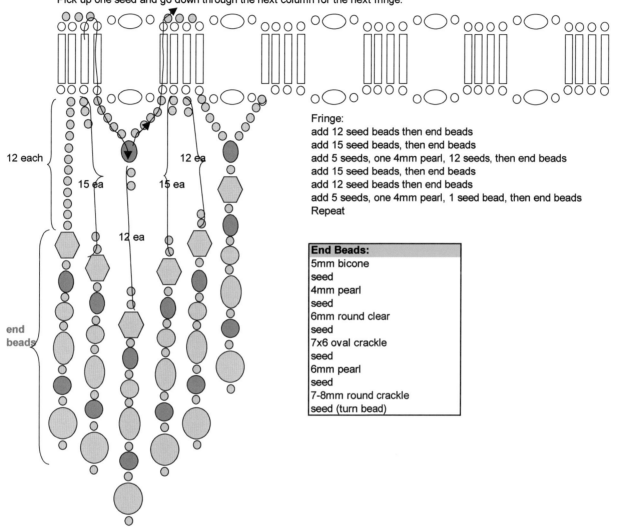

Fringe:
add 12 seed beads then end beads
add 15 seed beads, then end beads
add 5 seeds, one 4mm pearl, 12 seeds, then end beads
add 15 seed beads, then end beads
add 12 seed beads then end beads
add 5 seeds, one 4mm pearl, 1 seed bead, then end beads
Repeat

End Beads:
5mm bicone
seed
4mm pearl
seed
6mm round clear
seed
7x6 oval crackle
seed
6mm pearl
seed
7-8mm round crackle
seed (turn bead)

Fringed Ornament – Golden Ruby

Supplies:

25 grams sz 11 seed bead ambers amber transparent

1 gram sz 11 seed bead ambers red transparent matte

2 grams 6mm bugle beads twisted amber transparent AB

56 ea 4mm Czech Fire polish beads light amber transparent

56 ea 4mm Czech Fire polish beads ruby transparent

42 ea 14x1.5mm tube beads ruby transparent

42 ea 5mm bicone beads amber transparent

42 ea 6mm round beads amber transparent

42 ea 8mm round crackle glass beads amber

14 ea 10mm coin beads ruby

Beading thread size A Silamide or B Nymo beige/gold

Beading needle size 12

Glass ball ornament 2 ¾ diameter

Steps:

Make a strip that will go around the glass ball:

1. Cut 4 yards of thread and put a needle on one end to work single thread.
2. Use the "Half-thread Method" so add a Stop Bead with a 2 yard tail.   (Stop Bead see page 61) (Half Thread Method see page 62).
3. Pick up one seed bead amber, one bugle and one seed bead amber. Move down to the stop bead.
4. Pick up one seed bead amber, one bugle and one seed bead amber. Stitch through the previous column, then through the current column.

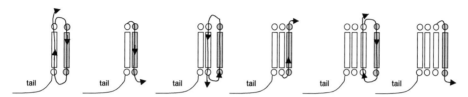

5. Repeat step 4 until there are 4 columns with bugles.
6. Pick up one seed bead amber, one 4mm amber, two seed bead ambers, one bugle, two seed bead ambers, one 4mm amber and one seed bead amber.
7. Stitch through the previous column, through the seed-4mm-seed, and the current column.

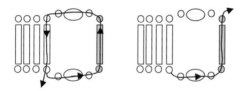

8. Repeat step 4 through 7, ending with step 5 until there is approximately 9 to 12 inches of thread left. Leave this thread end.
9. Remove the stop bead and add a needle to this tail end of the thread.
10. Repeat steps 4 through 7, starting at step 6. Stop when there are 13 sections of 4mm windows, ending

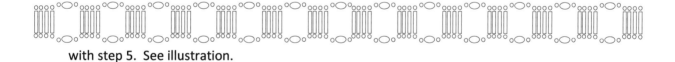

   with step 5. See illustration.

11. Stitch back through the strip, **all the way to the other end** to reinforce. Use the two threads and tie a square knot. Weave the ends in and cut.

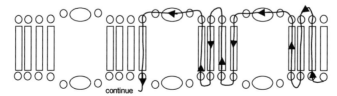

Add fringe to the strip:

12. Cut 3 yards of thread and put a needle on to work single thread. You will need to add a new thread, so if you would prefer to work with a shorter thread, feel free to do so.   See page 63 for instructions on adding new thread.

13. Add a Stop Bead with a 6 inch tail.
14. Stitch up through the end column on the strip (for right handers, the left-most end, for left-handers, do the right-most end). Pick up one seed bead amber and down through the next column.

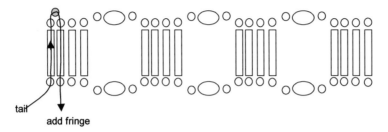

tail

add fringe

15. Create the fringe according to the Fringe Chart (at the end of the steps) until you get to the final column on the opposite end from where you started.
16. Close the strip into a circle: Pick up one seed bead amber, one 4mm amber, and one seed bead amber. Stitch up through the column on the starting end. Pick up one seed bead amber, one 4mm amber and one seed bead amber and stitch down through the current column.

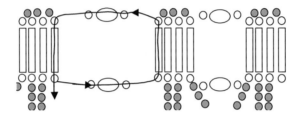

17. Repeat the thread path again to reinforce.
18. Create the final fringe.
19. Remove the stop bead and use the tail and needle threads to tie a square knot. Weave in the ends and cut.

Create the top section:
20. Cut 4 yards of thread and move the needle to the middle to work double thread.
21. Create a loop that will fit over the glass ball top. Use fourteen 4mm amber beads and use enough seeds to make the loop fit over the glass ball top. Pick up the beads and stitch through them again, then pull to create a loop. Tie a square knot. Leave the tail threads (used later for another knot).

pick up: 4mm,seed,4mm,seed,4mm,seed,4mm,4mm,seed,4mm,seed,4mm,seed,4mm, 4mm, seed,
4mm, seed, 4mm, 4mm, seed, 4mm, seed, 4mm

tail

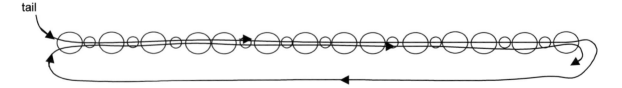

22. Pick up three seeds , one 4mm ruby, three seeds, one coin, and four seeds. Stitch through the seed-4mm-seed section on the fringed strip. Pick up four seeds , one coin, and three seeds. Stitch up through the first 4mm added. Pick up three seeds and stitch through the 4mm in the top loop over to and through the next 4mm on the top loop.

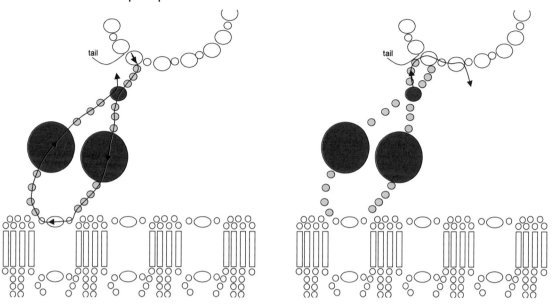

23. Pick up three seeds, one 4mm ruby, three seeds, one coin, and four seeds. Stitch through the seed-4mm-seed on the fringed strip below. Pick up four seeds and stitch through the coin on the previous section.

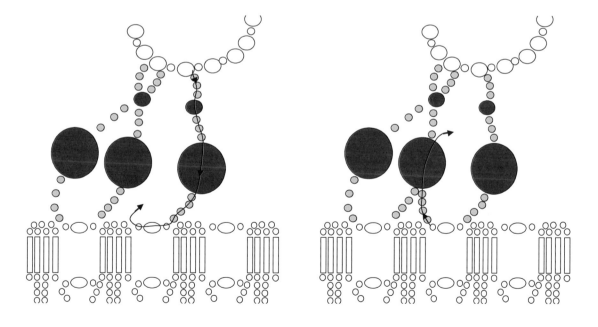

24. Pick up three seeds and stitch through the first added 4mm on this section. Pick up three seeds and through the 4mm in the loop above and over to and through the next 4mm on the top loop.

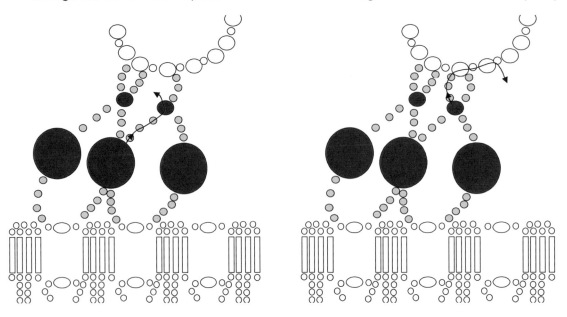

25. Repeat steps 23 and 24 until you are on the last 4mm in the top loop.

26. Pick up three seeds, one 4mm ruby and three seeds. Stitch through the coin in the first added section. Pick up four seeds and stitch through the seed-4mm-seed on the fringed strip below. Pick up four seeds and stitch through the coin in the previous section.

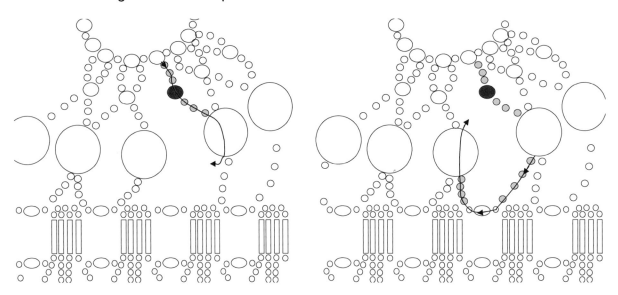

27. Pick up three seeds and stitch up through the 4mm added previously. Pick up three seeds and stitch through the 4mm above on the loop over to the tail thread.

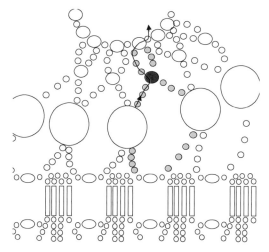

28. Use the tail threads and needle thread and tie a square knot.

29. Weave the ends in by stitching through the top loop with the needle threads in one direction and the tail threads in the opposite direction. Pull tightly and maneuver so the knot is pulled inside the 4mm bead. Cut the threads.

Fringe Chart

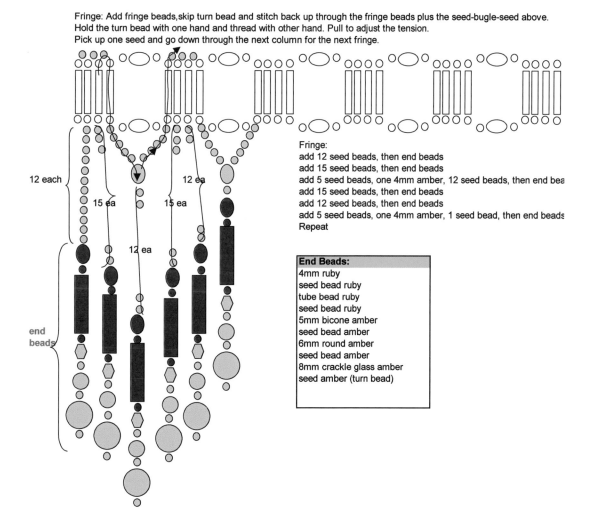

Fringe: Add fringe beads, skip turn bead and stitch back up through the fringe beads plus the seed-bugle-seed above.
Hold the turn bead with one hand and thread with other hand. Pull to adjust the tension.
Pick up one seed and go down through the next column for the next fringe.

12 each

15 ea

15 ea

12 ea

end beads

Fringe:
add 12 seed beads, then end beads
add 15 seed beads, then end beads
add 5 seed beads, one 4mm amber, 12 seed beads, then end bea
add 15 seed beads, then end beads
add 12 seed beads, then end beads
add 5 seed beads, one 4mm amber, 1 seed bead, then end beads
Repeat

End Beads:
4mm ruby
seed bead ruby
tube bead ruby
seed bead ruby
5mm bicone amber
seed bead amber
6mm round amber
seed bead amber
8mm crackle glass amber
seed amber (turn bead)

Fringed Ornament – Spring Wine

Supplies:

18 grams sz 11 seed beads light green transparent

8 grams sz 11 seed beads light amethyst AB matte

2 grams 6mm bugle beads twisted light green transparent AB

56 ea 4mm Czech Fire polish silver/green

112 ea 4mm Czech Fire polish light amethyst

42 ea 14x4.5mm tube beads light amethyst transparent

42 ea 9x5mm oval twist light amethyst transparent

42 ea 6mm Czech Fire polish beads silver/green

42 ea 8mm round light green crackle glass

Beading thread size A Silamide or B Nymo beige

Beading needle size 12

Glass ball ornament 2 ¾ diameter

Steps:

Make a strip that will go around the glass ball:

1. Cut 4 yards of thread and put a needle on one end to work single thread.
2. Use the "Half-thread Method" so add a Stop Bead with a 2 yard tail.   (Stop Bead see page 61) (Half Thread Method see page 62).
3. Pick up one seed green, one bugle and one seed green. Move down to the stop bead.
4. Pick up one seed green, one bugle and one seed green. Stitch through the previous column, then through the current column.

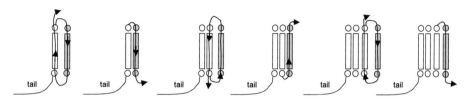

5. Repeat step 4 until there are 4 columns with bugles.
6. Pick up one seed amethyst, one 4mm amethyst, one seed amethyst, one seed green, one bugle, one seed green, one seed amethyst, one 4mm amethyst and one seed amethyst.
7. Stitch through the previous column, through the seed-4mm seed, and the current column.

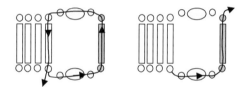

8. Repeat step 4 through 7, ending with step 5 until there is approximately 9 to 12 inches of thread left. Leave this thread end.
9. Remove the stop bead and add a needle to this tail end of the thread.
10. Repeat steps 4 through 7, starting at step 6. Stop when there are 13 sections of 4mm windows, ending with step 5. See illustration.

11. Stitch back through the strip, **all the way to the other end** to reinforce. Use the two threads and tie a square knot. Weave the ends in and cut.

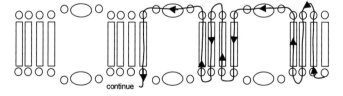

Add fringe to the strip:

12. Cut 3 yards of thread and put a needle on to work single thread. You will need to add a new thread, so if you would prefer to work with a shorter thread, feel free to do so. See page 63 for instructions on adding new thread.

---

13. Add a Stop Bead with a 6 inch tail.
14. Stitch up through the end column on the strip (for right handers, the left-most end, for left-handers, do the right-most end). Pick up one seed green and down through the next column.

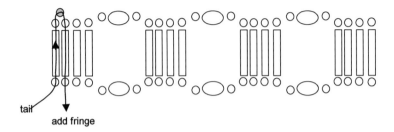

tail
add fringe

15. Create the fringe according to the Fringe Chart (at the end of the steps) until you get to the final column on the opposite end from where you started.
16. Close the strip into a circle: Pick up one seed amethyst, one 4mm amethyst, and one seed amethyst. Stitch up through the column on the starting end. Pick up one seed amethyst, one 4mm amethyst and one seed amethyst and stitch down through the current column.

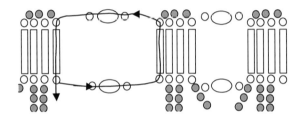

17. Repeat the thread path again to reinforce.
18. Create the final fringe.
19. Remove the stop bead. Use the tail and needle threads to tie a square knot. Weave in the ends and cut.

Create the top section (see Fitting the Ball page 63):
20. Cut 4 yards of thread and move the needle to the middle to work double thread.
21. Create a loop that will fit over the glass ball top. Use fourteen 4mm green beads and use enough green seeds to make the loop fit over the glass ball top. Pick up the beads and stitch through them again, then pull to create a loop. Tie a square knot. Leave the tail threads (used later for another knot).

pick up: 4mm,seed,4mm,seed,4mm,seed,4mm,4mm,seed,4mm,seed,4mm,seed,4mm, 4mm, seed,
4mm, seed, 4mm, 4mm, seed, 4mm, seed, 4mm

tail

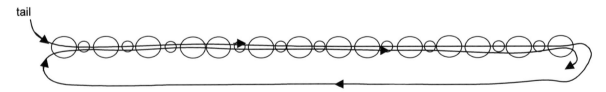

22. Pick up three seeds green, one 4mm amethyst, five seeds amethyst, one 4mm amethyst, one 4mm green, six seeds green. Stitch through the seed-4mm-seed section on the fringed strip. Pick up six seeds green,

one 4mm green, one 4mm amethyst, and five seeds amethyst. Stitch up through the first 4mm added. Pick up three seeds green and stitch through the 4mm in the top loop over to and through the next 4mm on the top loop.

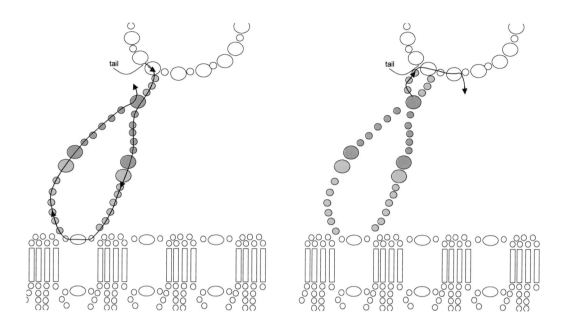

23. Pick up three seeds green, one 4mm amethyst, five seeds amethyst, one 4mm amethyst, one 4mm green, and six seeds green. Stitch through the seed-4mm-seed on the fringed strip below. Pick up six seeds green and stitch through the two 4mm beads on the previous section.

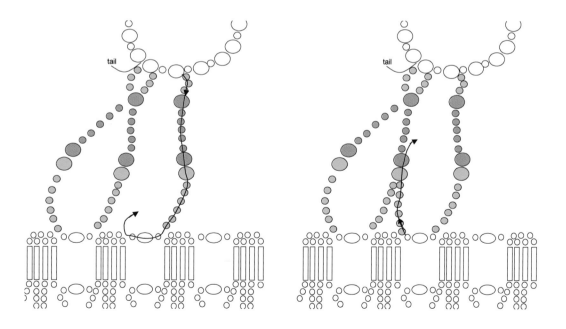

24. Pick up five seeds amethyst and stitch through the first added 4mm on this section. Pick up three seeds green and through the 4mm in the loop above and over to and through the next 4mm on the top loop.

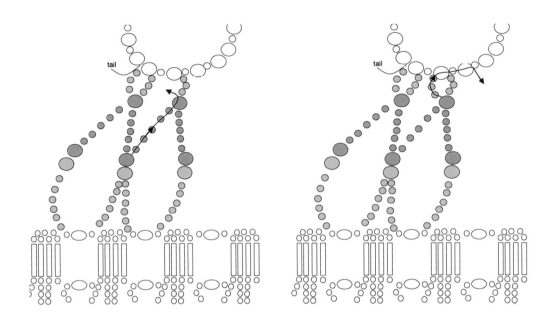

25. Repeat steps 23 and 24 until you are on the last 4mm in the top loop.
26. Pick up three seeds green, one 4mm amethyst and five seeds amethyst. Stitch through the two 4mm beads in the first added section. Pick up six seeds green and stitch through the seed-4mm-seed on the fringed strip below. Pick up 6 seeds green and stitch through the two 4mm beads in the previous section.

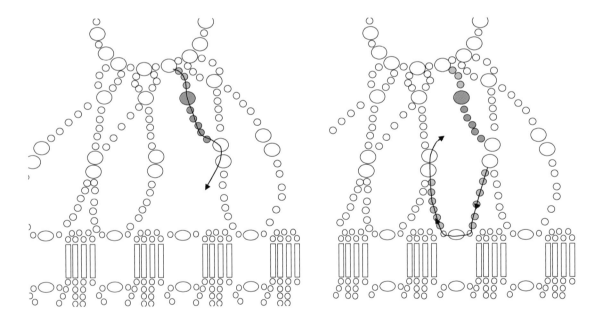

27. Pick up 5 seeds amethyst and stitch up through the 4mm added previously. Pick up three seeds green and stitch through the 4mm above on the loop over to the tail thread.

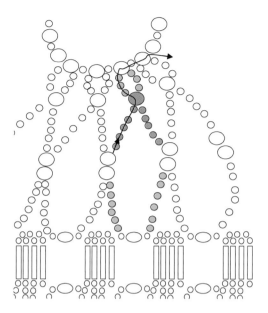

28. Use the tail threads and needle thread and tie a square knot.
29. Weave the ends in by stitching through the top loop with the needle threads in one direction and the tail threads in the opposite direction. Pull tightly and maneuver so the knot is pulled inside the 4mm bead. Cut the threads.
30. Cut 1 yard of thread and put a needle on to work single thread.
31. Add a stop bead with a 6 inch tail.
32. Stitch up through one seed above the 4mm on the top section and down through the seed next to it.
33. Pick up three seeds amethyst, one 4mm amethyst, one 4mm green and one seed green(turn bead). Stitch back through the added 4mm beads and hold the turn bead and pull to adjust the tension. Pick up three seeds amethyst and stitch up through the seed on top of the 4mm in the next section. Stitch down through the seed next to it.

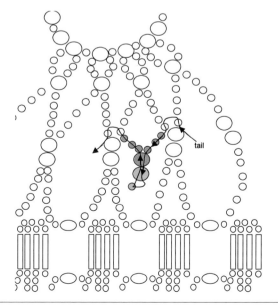

34. Repeat step 33 to return to the start.
35. Remove the stop bead. Use the tail thread and needle thread and tie a square knot. Weave the ends in and cut.
36. Done!

Fringe Chart:

Fringe: Add fringe beads, skip turn bead and stitch back up through the fringe beads plus the seed-bugle-seed above. Hold the turn bead with one hand and thread with other hand. Pull to adjust the tension.
Pick up one seed and go down through the next column for the next fringe.

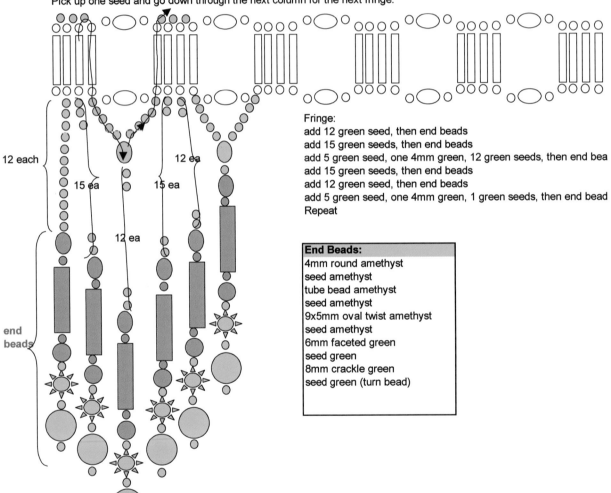

12 each

15 ea

12 ea

15 ea

12 ea

end beads

Fringe:
add 12 green seed, then end beads
add 15 green seeds, then end beads
add 5 green seed, one 4mm green, 12 green seeds, then end bea
add 15 green seeds, then end beads
add 12 green seed, then end beads
add 5 green seed, one 4mm green, 1 green seeds, then end bead
Repeat

End Beads:
4mm round amethyst
seed amethyst
tube bead amethyst
seed amethyst
9x5mm oval twist amethyst
seed amethyst
6mm faceted green
seed green
8mm crackle green
seed green (turn bead)

Fringed Ornament – Ice Blue

Supplies:

25 grams sz 11 seed beads light blue AB

2 grams 6mm bugle beads twisted light blue AB

126 ea 4mm Czech Fire polish beads silver

42 ea 4mm round beads light blue transparent

42 ea 6mm round beads silver polished

42 ea 5mm bicone beads silver polished

42 ea 6mm Czech Fire polish beads light blue

42 ea 8mm round crackle glass beads light blue

14 ea 11x9mm butterfly beads silver polished

Beading thread size A Silamide or B Nymo light blue/white

Beading needle size 12

Glass ball ornament 2 ¾ diameter

Steps:

Make a strip that will go around the glass ball:

1. Cut 4 yards of thread and put a needle on one end to work single thread.
2. Use the "Half-thread Method" so add a Stop Bead with a 2 yard tail.   (Stop Bead see page 61) (Half Thread Method see page 62).
3. Pick up one seed bead, one bugle and one seed bead. Move down to the stop bead.
4. Pick up one seed bead, one bugle and one seed bead. Stitch through the previous column, then through the current column.

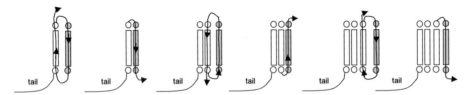

5. Repeat step 4 until there are 4 columns with bugles.
6. Pick up one seed bead, one 4mm silver, two seed beads, one bugle, two seed beads, one 4mm silver and one seed bead.
7. Stitch through the previous column, through the seed-4mm-seed, and the current column.

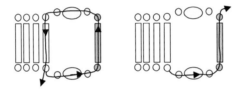

8. Repeat step 4 through 7, ending with step 5 until there is approximately 9 to 12 inches of thread left. Leave this thread end.
9. Remove the stop bead and add a needle to this tail end of the thread.
10. Repeat steps 4 through 7, starting at step 6. Stop when there are 13 sections of 4mm windows, ending with step 5. See illustration.

11. Stitch back through the strip, **all the way to the other end** to reinforce. Use the two threads and tie a square knot. Weave the ends in and cut.

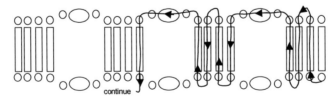

Add fringe to the strip:

12. Cut 3 yards of thread and put a needle on to work single thread. You will need to add a new thread, so if you would prefer to work with a shorter thread, feel free to do so. See page 63 for instructions on adding new thread.

13. Add a Stop Bead with a 6 inch tail.
14. Stitch up through the end column on the strip (for right handers, the left-most end, for left-handers, do the right-most end). Pick up one seed bead and down through the next column.

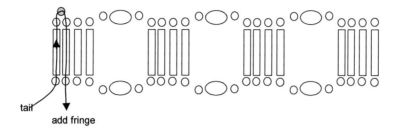

15. Create the fringe according to the Fringe Chart (at the end of the steps) until you get to the final column on the opposite end from where you started.
16. Close the strip into a circle: Pick up one seed bead, one 4mm silver, and one seed bead. Stitch up through the column on the starting end. Pick up one seed bead, one 4mm silver and one seed bead and stitch down through the current column.

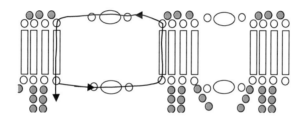

17. Repeat the thread path again to reinforce.
18. Create the final fringe.
19. Remove the stop bead. Use the tail and needle threads to tie a square knot. Weave in the ends and cut.

Create the top section (see Fitting the Ball page 63):
20. Cut 4 yards of thread and move the needle to the middle to work double thread.
21. Create a loop that will fit over the glass ball top. Use fourteen 4mm blue beads and use enough seeds to make the loop fit over the glass ball top. Pick up the beads and stitch through them again, then pull to create a loop. Tie a square knot. Leave the tail threads (used later for another knot).

pick up: 4mm,seed,4mm,seed,4mm,seed,4mm,4mm,seed,4mm,seed,4mm,seed,4mm, 4mm, seed,
4mm, seed, 4mm, 4mm, seed, 4mm, seed, 4mm

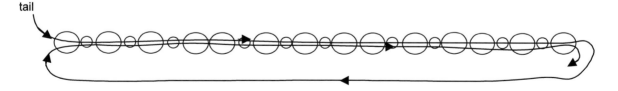

22. Pick up three seeds , one 4mm silver, five seeds, one 4mm blue, one butterfly, and five seeds. Stitch through the seed-4mm-seed section on the fringed strip. Pick up five seeds , one butterfly, one 4mm blue, and five seeds. Stitch up through the first 4mm added. Pick up three seeds and stitch through the 4mm in the top loop over to and through the next 4mm on the top loop.

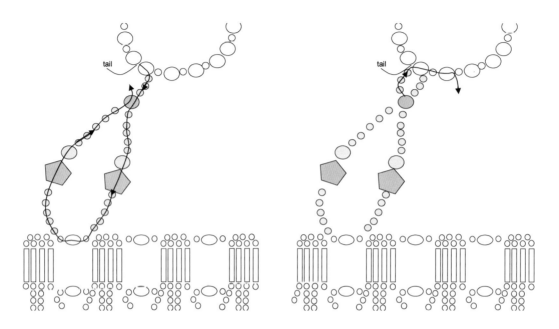

23. Pick up three seeds, one 4mm silver, five seeds, one 4mm blue, one butterfly, and five seeds. Stitch through the seed-4mm-seed on the fringed strip below. Pick up five seeds and stitch through the butterfly and 4mm on the previous section.

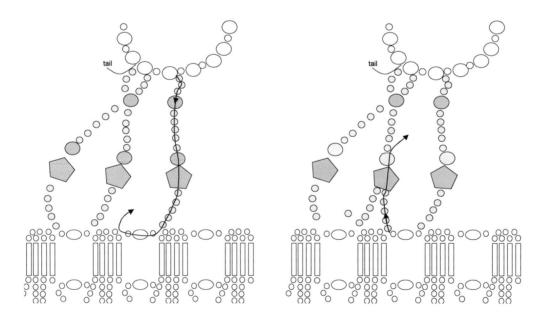

24. Pick up five seeds and stitch through the first added 4mm on this section. Pick up three seeds and through the 4mm in the loop above and over to and through the next 4mm on the top loop.

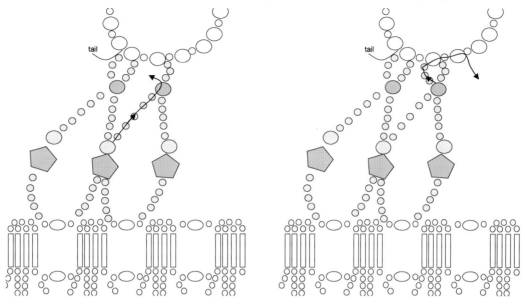

25. Repeat steps 23 and 24 until you are on the last 4mm in the top loop.

26. Pick up three seeds, one 4mm silver and five seeds. Stitch through the 4mm bead and butterfly in the first added section. Pick up five seeds and stitch through the seed-4mm-seed on the fringed strip below. Pick up five seeds and stitch through the butterfly and 4mm bead in the previous section.

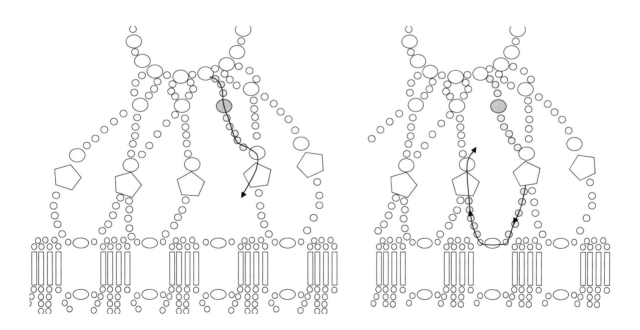

27. Pick up 5 seeds and stitch up through the 4mm added previously. Pick up three seeds and stitch through the 4mm above on the loop over to the tail thread.

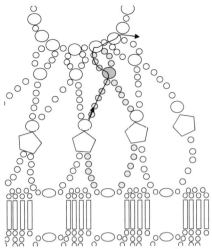

Use the tail threads and needle thread and tie a square knot.

28. Weave the ends in by stitching through the top loop with the needle threads in one direction and the tail threads in the opposite direction. Pull tightly and maneuver so the knot is pulled inside the 4mm bead. Cut the threads. Done!

Fringe Chart

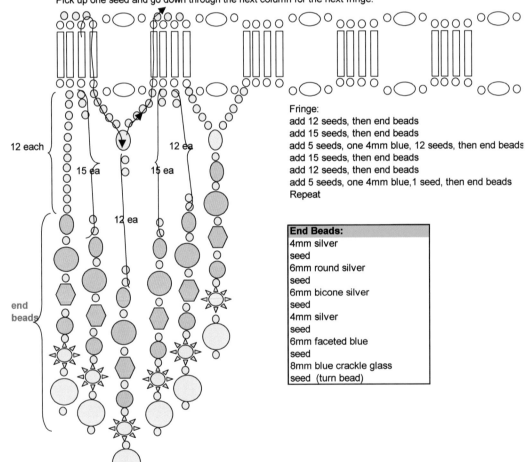

Fringe: Add fringe beads, skip turn bead and stitch back up through the fringe beads plus the seed-bugle-seed
Hold the turn bead with one hand and thread with other hand. Pull to adjust the tension.
Pick up one seed and go down through the next column for the next fringe.

Fringe:
add 12 seeds, then end beads
add 15 seeds, then end beads
add 5 seeds, one 4mm blue, 12 seeds, then end beads
add 15 seeds, then end beads
add 12 seeds, then end beads
add 5 seeds, one 4mm blue,1 seed, then end beads
Repeat

End Beads:
4mm silver
seed
6mm round silver
seed
6mm bicone silver
seed
4mm silver
seed
6mm faceted blue
seed
8mm blue crackle glass
seed (turn bead)

Fringed Ornament – Black Tie Affair

Supplies:

18 grams sz 11 seed beads black opaque

8 grams sz 11 seed beads gold lined crystal

2 grams 6mm bugle beads black opaque

70 ea 4mm Czech Fire polish black opaque

84 ea 4mm Czech Fire polish gold metallic

98 ea 4mm round gold metallic

42 ea 14x4.5mm tube beads black opaque

42 ea 5mm round bicone black opaque

42 ea 6mm round black opaque

42 ea 8mm Czech Fire polish black opaque

Beading thread size A Silamide or B Nymo black

Beading needle size 12

Glass ball ornament 2 5/8 diameter

Steps:

Make a strip that will go around the glass ball:

1. Cut 4 yards of thread and put a needle on one end to work single thread.
2. Use the "Half-thread Method" so add a Stop Bead with a 2 yard tail. (Stop Bead see page 61) (Half Thread Method see page 62).
3. Pick up one seed black, one bugle and one seed black. Move down to the stop bead.
4. Pick up one seed black, one bugle and one seed black. Stitch through the previous column, then through the current column.

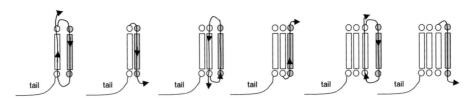

5. Repeat step 4 until there are 4 columns with bugles.
6. Pick up one seed gold, one 4mm fire polish gold, one seed gold, one seed black, one bugle, one seed black, one seed gold, one 4mm fire polish gold and one seed gold.
7. Stitch through the previous column, through the seed-4mm seed, and the current column.

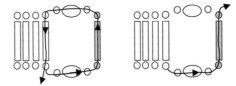

8. Repeat step 4 through 7, ending with step 5 until there is approximately 9 to 12 inches of thread left. Leave this thread end.
9. Remove the stop bead and add a needle to this tail end of the thread.
10. Repeat steps 4 through 7, starting at step 6. Stop when there are 13 sections of 4mm windows, ending with step 5. See illustration.

11. Stitch back through the strip, **all the way to the other end** to reinforce. Use the two threads and tie a square knot. Weave the ends in and cut.

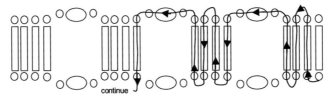

Add fringe to the strip:

12. Cut 3 yards of thread and put a needle on to work single thread. You will need to add a new thread, so if you would prefer to work with a shorter thread, feel free to do so. See page 63 for instructions on adding new thread.
13. Add a Stop Bead with a 6 inch tail.

14. Stitch up through the end column on the strip (for right handers, the left-most end, for left-handers, do the right-most end). Pick up one seed black and stitch down through the next column.

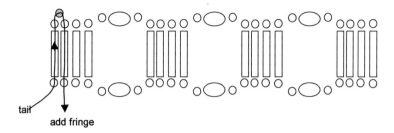

tail

add fringe

15. Create the fringe according to the Fringe Chart (at the end of the steps) until you get to the final column on the opposite end from where you started.

16. Close the strip into a circle: Pick up one seed gold, one 4mm fire polish gold, and one seed gold. Stitch up through the column on the starting end. Pick up one seed gold, one 4mm fire polish gold and one seed gold and stitch down through the current column.

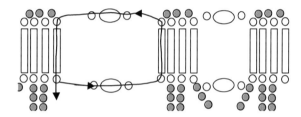

17. Repeat the thread path again to reinforce.
18. Create the final fringe.
19. Remove the stop bead. Use the tail and needle threads to tie a square knot. Weave in the ends and cut.

Create the top section:

20. Cut 4 yards of thread and move the needle to the middle to work double thread.
21. Create a loop that will fit over the glass ball top. Use fourteen 4mm black beads and use enough black seeds to make the loop fit over the glass ball top. Pick up the beads and stitch through them again, then pull to create a loop. Tie a square knot. Leave the tail threads (used later for another knot).

pick up: 4mm,seed,4mm,seed,4mm,seed,4mm,4mm,seed,4mm,seed,4mm,seed,4mm, 4mm, seed, 4mm, seed, 4mm, 4mm, seed, 4mm, seed, 4mm

tail

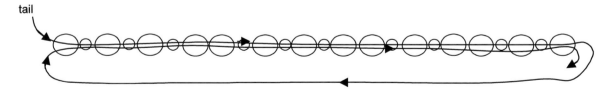

22. Pick up three seeds black, one 4mm fire polish black, five seeds gold, two 4mm's black, six seeds black. Stitch through the seed-4mm-seed section on the fringed strip. Pick up six seeds black, two 4mm's black,

and five seeds gold. Stitch up through the first 4mm added. Pick up three seeds black and stitch through the 4mm in the top loop over to and through the next 4mm on the top loop.

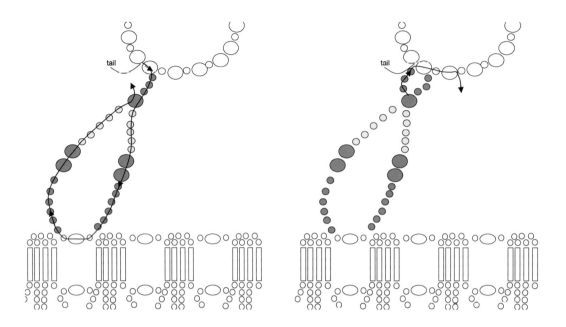

23. Pick up three seeds black, one 4mm black, five seeds gold, two 4mm's black, and six seeds black. Stitch through the seed-4mm-seed on the fringed strip below. Pick up six seeds black and stitch through the two 4mm beads on the previous section.

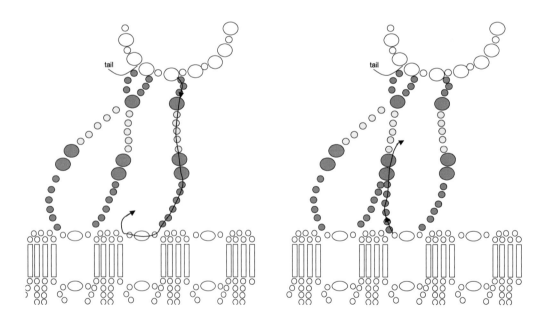

24. Pick up five seeds gold and stitch through the first added 4mm on this section. Pick up three seeds black and through the 4mm in the loop above and over to and through the next 4mm on the top loop.

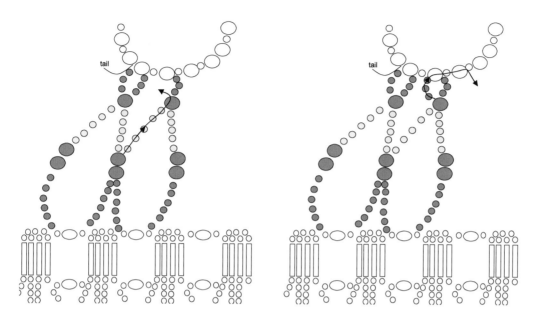

25. Repeat steps 23 and 24 until you are on the last 4mm in the top loop.

26. Pick up three seeds black, one 4mm black and five seeds gold. Stitch through the two 4mm beads in the first added section. Pick up six seeds black and stitch through the seed-4mm-seed on the fringed strip below. Pick up 6 seeds black and stitch through the two 4mm beads in the previous section.

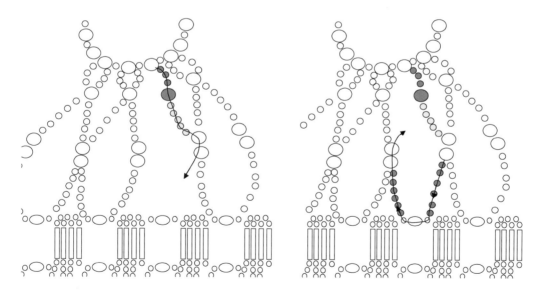

27. Pick up 5 seeds gold and stitch up through the 4mm added previously. Pick up three seeds black and stitch through the 4mm above on the loop over to the tail thread.

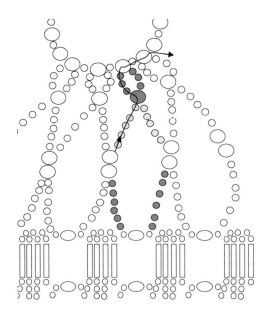

28. Use the tail threads and needle thread and tie a square knot.

29. Weave the ends in by stitching through the top loop with the needle threads in one direction and the tail threads in the opposite direction. Pull tightly and maneuver so the knot is pulled inside the 4mm bead. Cut the threads.

30. Cut 1 yard of thread and put a needle on to work single thread.

31. Add a stop bead with a 6 inch tail.

32. Stitch up through one seed above the 4mm on the top section and down through the seed next to it.

33. Pick up three seeds gold, one 4mm fire polish gold, one 4mm round gold and one seed gold (turn bead). Stitch back through the added 4mm beads and hold the turn bead and pull to adjust the tension. Pick up three seeds gold and stitch up through the seed on top of the 4mm in the next section. Stitch down through the seed next to it.

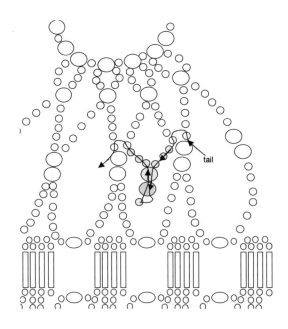

34. Repeat step 33 to return to the start.
35. Remove the stop bead. Use the tail thread and needle thread and tie a square knot. Weave the ends in and cut.
36. Done!

Fringe Chart:

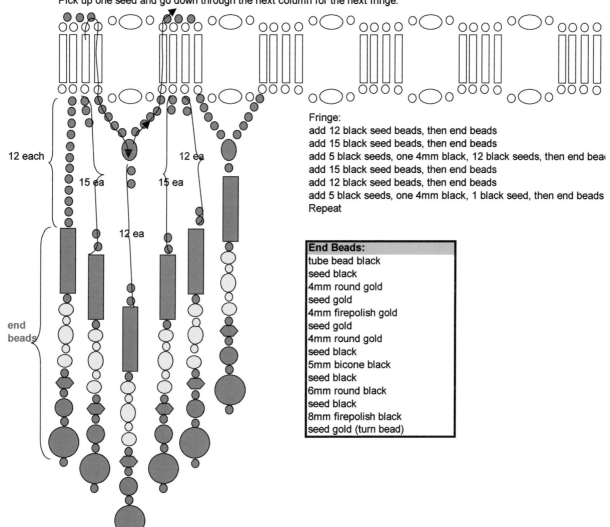

Fringe: Add fringe beads, skip turn bead and stitch back up through the fringe beads plus the seed-bugle-seed above. Hold the turn bead with one hand and thread with other hand. Pull to adjust the tension. Pick up one seed and go down through the next column for the next fringe.

12 each

15 ea

12 ea

12 ea

15 ea

12 ea

end beads

Fringe:
add 12 black seed beads, then end beads
add 15 black seed beads, then end beads
add 5 black seeds, one 4mm black, 12 black seeds, then end bead
add 15 black seed beads, then end beads
add 12 black seed beads, then end beads
add 5 black seeds, one 4mm black, 1 black seed, then end beads
Repeat

End Beads:
tube bead black
seed black
4mm round gold
seed gold
4mm firepolish gold
seed gold
4mm round gold
seed black
5mm bicone black
seed black
6mm round black
seed black
8mm firepolish black
seed gold (turn bead)

Fringed Ornament – Rainbow

Supplies:

10 grams sz 11 seed beads turquoise

10 grams sz 11 seed beads green

2 grams sz 11 seed beads orange

2 grams sz 11 seed beads yellow

2 grams sz 11 seed beads pink

2 grams 6mm bugle beads twisted turquoise transparent AB

56 ea 4mm Czech Fire polish pink

14 ea 4mm Czech Fire polish orange

70 ea 4mm Czech Fire polish yellow

70 ea 4mm Czech Fire polish green

42 ea 6mm round pink crackle glass

42 ea 7x4mm tube beads orange

42 ea 6mm fluted round yellow

42 ea 5mm bicone green

42 ea 7mm cube beads green

42 ea 8mm round turquoise crackle glass

Beading thread size A Silamide or B Nymo white

Beading needle size 12

Glass ball ornament 2 5/8 diameter

Steps:

Make a strip that will go around the glass ball:

1. Cut 4 yards of thread and put a needle on one end to work single thread.
2. Use the "Half-thread Method" so add a Stop Bead with a 2 yard tail.   (Stop Bead see page 61) (Half Thread Method see page 62).
3. Pick up one seed turquoise, one bugle and one seed turquoise. Move down to the stop bead.
4. Pick up one seed turquoise, one bugle and one seed turquoise. Stitch through the previous column, then through the current column.

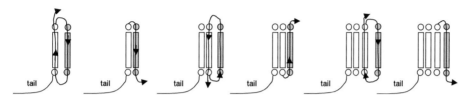

5. Repeat step 4 until there are 4 columns with bugles.
6. Pick up one seed green, one 4mm green, one seed green, one seed turquoise, one bugle, one seed turquoise, one seed green, one 4mm green and one seed green.
7. Stitch through the previous column, through the seed-4mm seed, and the current column.

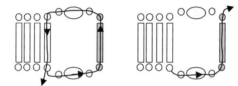

8. Repeat step 4 through 7, ending with step 5 until there is approximately 9 to 12 inches of thread left. Leave this thread end.
9. Remove the stop bead and add a needle to this tail end of the thread.
10. Repeat steps 4 through 7, starting at step 6. Stop when there are 13 sections of 4mm windows, ending with step 5. See illustration.

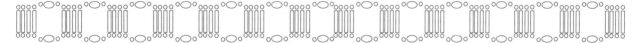

11. Stitch back through the strip, **all the way to the other end** to reinforce. Use the two threads and tie a square knot. Weave the ends in and cut.

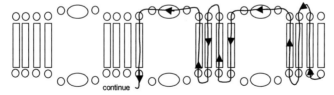

Add fringe to the strip:

12. Cut 3 yards of thread and put a needle on to work single thread. You will need to add a new thread, so if you would prefer to work with a shorter thread, feel free to do so. See page 63 for instructions on adding new thread.
13. Add a Stop Bead with a 6 inch tail.

14. Stitch up through the end column on the strip (for right handers, the left-most end, for left-handers, do the right-most end). Pick up one seed turquoise and down through the next column.

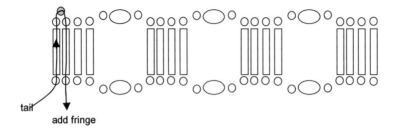

tail

add fringe

15. Create the fringe according to the Fringe Chart (at the end of the steps) until you get to the final column on the opposite end from where you started.
16. Close the strip into a circle: Pick up one seed green, one 4mm green, and one seed green. Stitch up through the column on the starting end. Pick up one seed green, one 4mm green and one seed green and stitch down through the current column.

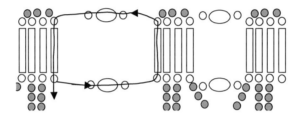

17. Repeat the thread path again to reinforce.
18. Create the final fringe.
19. Remove the stop bead. Use the tail and needle threads to tie a square knot. Weave in the ends and cut.

Create the top section:
20. Cut 4 yards of thread and move the needle to the middle to work double thread.
21. Create a loop that will fit over the glass ball top. Use fourteen 4mm pink beads and use enough pink seeds to make the loop fit over the glass ball top. Pick up the beads and stitch through them again, then pull to create a loop. Tie a square knot. Leave the tail threads (used later for another knot).

pick up: 4mm,seed,4mm,seed,4mm,seed,4mm,4mm,seed,4mm,seed,4mm,seed,4mm, 4mm, seed, 4mm, seed, 4mm, 4mm, seed, 4mm, seed, 4mm

tail

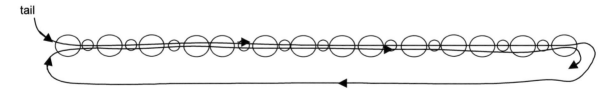

22. Pick up three seeds pink, one 4mm orange, five seeds orange, two 4mm green, and six seeds green. Stitch through the seed-4mm-seed section on the fringed strip. Pick up six seeds green, two 4mm green, and

five seeds orange. Stitch up through the first 4mm added. Pick up three seeds pink and stitch through the 4mm in the top loop over to and through the next 4mm on the top loop.

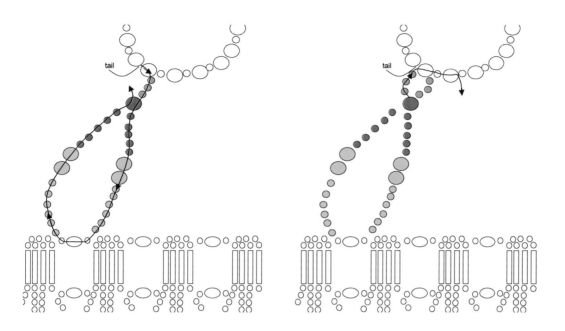

23. Pick up three seeds pink, one 4mm orange, five seeds orange, two 4mm green, and six seeds green. Stitch through the seed-4mm-seed on the fringed strip below. Pick up six seeds green and stitch through the two 4mm beads on the previous section.

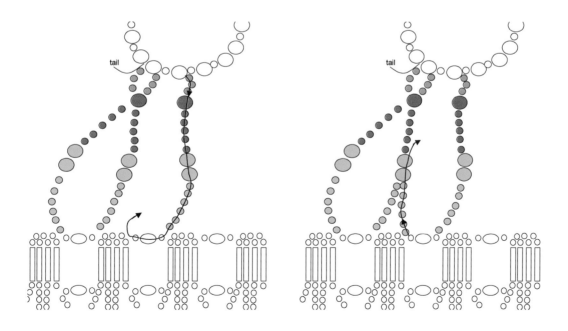

24. Pick up five seeds orange and stitch through the first added 4mm on this section. Pick up three seeds pink and through the 4mm in the loop above and over to and through the next 4mm on the top loop.

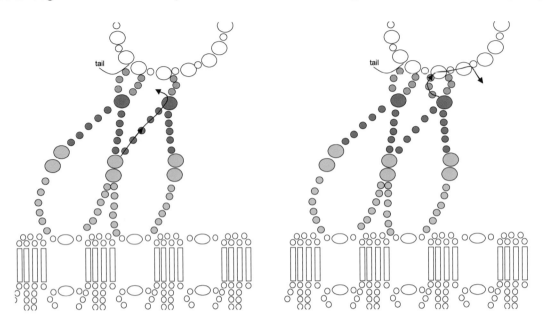

25. Repeat steps 23 and 24 until you are on the last 4mm in the top loop.
26. Pick up three seeds pink, one 4mm orange and five seeds orange. Stitch through the two 4mm beads in the first added section. Pick up six seeds green and stitch through the seed-4mm-seed on the fringed strip below. Pick up 6 seeds green and stitch through the two 4mm beads in the previous section.

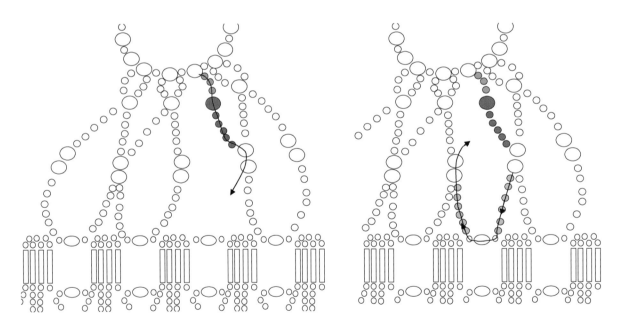

27. Pick up 5 seeds orange and stitch up through the 4mm added previously. Pick up three seeds pink and stitch through the 4mm above on the loop over to the tail thread.

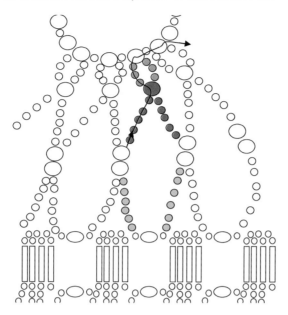

28. Use the tail threads and needle thread and tie a square knot.
29. Weave the ends in by stitching through the top loop with the needle threads in one direction and the tail threads in the opposite direction. Pull tightly and maneuver so the knot is pulled inside the 4mm bead. Cut the threads.
30. Cut 1 yard of thread and put a needle on to work single thread.
31. Add a stop bead with a 6 inch tail.
32. Stitch up through one seed above the 4mm on the top section and down through the seed next to it.
33. Pick up three seeds yellow, two 4mm yellow and one seed yellow (turn bead). Stitch back through the added 4mm beads and hold the turn bead and pull to adjust the tension. Pick up three seeds yellow and stitch up through the seed on top of the 4mm in the next section. Stitch down through the seed next to it.

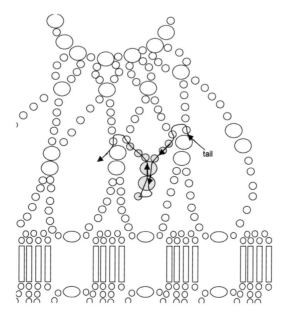

34. Repeat step 33 to return to the start.
35. Remove the stop bead. Use the tail thread and needle thread and tie a square knot. Weave the ends in and cut.
36. Done!

Fringe Chart:

Fringe: Add fringe beads, skip turn bead and stitch back up through the fringe beads plus the seed-bugle-seed above. Hold the turn bead with one hand and thread with other hand. Pull to adjust the tension.
Pick up one seed and go down through the next column for the next fringe.

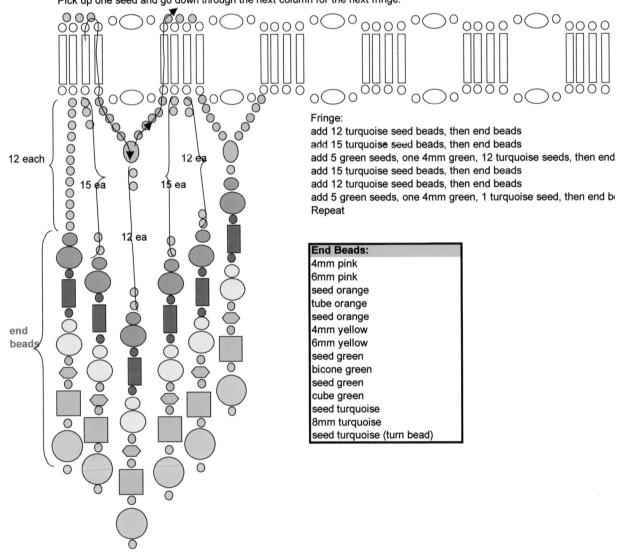

12 each

15 ea   15 ea

12 ea

12 ea

end beads

Fringe:
add 12 turquoise seed beads, then end beads
add 15 turquoise seed beads, then end beads
add 5 green seeds, one 4mm green, 12 turquoise seeds, then end
add 15 turquoise seed beads, then end beads
add 12 turquoise seed beads, then end beads
add 5 green seeds, one 4mm green, 1 turquoise seed, then end be
Repeat

End Beads:
4mm pink
6mm pink
seed orange
tube orange
seed orange
4mm yellow
6mm yellow
seed green
bicone green
seed green
cube green
seed turquoise
8mm turquoise
seed turquoise (turn bead)

Supplies and Basics

Seed Beads/Bugle Beads

Seed beads, small glass beads named for the seeds they resemble, are used throughout the projects. These beads are round in appearance and are also referred to as rocailles. Seed beads are sized according to number, the higher the number the smaller the bead. The most common size seed bead is size 11. The projects in this book use a rocaille (round) seed bead versus the other seed beads shaped like a tube or cylinder (generally referred to as Delicas or Tohos). You can substitute using the cylindrical beads, but this will affect the final look of the ornament. Generally, Japanese seed beads work better because the size of the holes is more consistent and larger than a Czech seed bead. Czech seed beads are usually sold in "Hanks" (temporarily strung beads tied together in a bunch) while Japanese seed beads are sold by the ounce in containers/bags. Ask your supplier if the beads are not labeled. The supplies lists detail the ounces needed, so, for conversion keep in mind that one hank of sz 11 seeds is approximately 40 grams. For the bugle beads, usually Czech beads are as good as the Japanese bugles, especially the Ornela brand of Czech bugles.

Needles/Thread

All of the projects in this book use needles and thread. The needles and thread are specifically made for beading and are thinner and stronger than those used for sewing. Beading needles come in sizes 10, 12, 13, and up, the higher the number, the smaller the needle. I recommend needles made in England (John James brand is great) because the size of the hole used to thread is larger in relation to the size of the needle. Beading thread comes in various colors and materials. The two most used are Nymo and Silamide. Each of these work very well and which to use is generally a personal preference. Threads are sized with an alphabetic designation such as A, B, C, O, etc. Nymo is selected by many beaders since it is usually easier to thread the needle with.

All of the projects in this book use size 12 needles and size A thread.

Beading Pad

Made specifically for beading, these pads are like a fleece blanket with a nap like that of velvet. The pad provides a cushion that allows you to pour out small piles of beads that stay in place without rolling around. The beads sit on top of the fibers and are easy to pick up with a needle.

Wax/Thread Conditioners

Beeswax and other thread conditioners (Thread Heaven, etc.) are used by many beaders. These products are applied to the bead thread to make it more manageable. Some threads (Silamide) are pre-waxed and therefore do not need any additional products.

Lamps

Good lighting is important for your comfort while beading. A small lamp where the light can be directed at the work area is recommended. There are many lamps made especially for beaders, many with "true color" light bulbs.

Scissors

Scissors with sharp blades and a small size for easy handling make a great addition to a beading tool chest.

Basic Techniques:
Add a Stop bead-

Starting a project of beadwork often involves leaving the tail thread for use later in completing the beadwork. Accordingly, there are no beginning knots to hold the tension. The use of a "Stop Bead" compensates for this and helps to hold the tension in the thread. The stop bead is a bead that is used temporarily and is removed later. The best stop bead is a size 8 or 9 bead in a matte finish because the roughness of the matte finish helps to hold the thread better and it is a large enough bead to easily remove later. However, any bead can be used as a stop bead. To add a stop bead, pick up the stop bead. Move it to the desired location and stitch through it again so the thread is looped around the bead. When you stitch in the bead again, be careful not to stitch through the thread already in the bead since that will cause problems when you try to remove it later. Pull the thread so the loop is tightly around the bead.

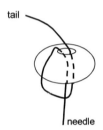

Knots-
Knots are used at the end of stitching to secure threads before they are cut. There are two situations for knots. One is when two thread ends are available to perform a knot, the other is when only one thread is available.

Square Knot: (when 2 threads available)
This is a preferred situation since the knot is the most secure. When a square knot is knotted correctly, and when the ends are woven into the beadwork in opposite directions, any stress on the knot actually makes it tighter. To tie a square knot, position the thread ends so that they are exiting two different beads and one is to the right and the other is to the left. Loop the right over and around the left. Then take the thread that is now on the left and loop it over and around the right. Pull the ends to secure the knot. Take one end and weave into the beadwork in one direction. Take the other end and weave into the beadwork in the opposite direction (see Weaving below) then cut.

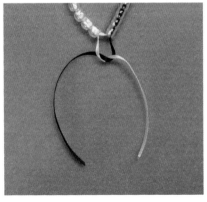 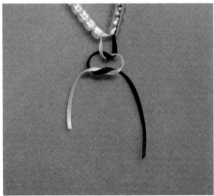

One-Thread Knot:

Stitch to an area in the beadwork where there are two threads coming out of a bead into two different directions. Stitch under the two threads and create pull gently to create a loop. Stitch through the loop, then through the loop again. Pull slowly to close the loops. Pull tight. Weave in (see below), then cut.

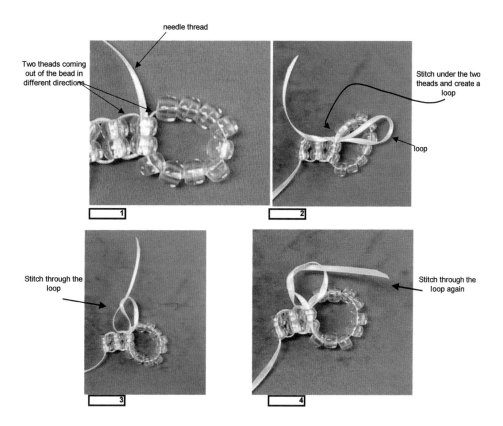

Weaving into beadwork: Always cut thread away from the knot, not next to it. Weave into the beadwork before cutting the thread. Fabric weavers have discovered that weaving threads back in, actually eliminates the need for knots if the weaving is done up then down then up then down. Weaving done in this back and forth pattern will secure the thread without the need for a knot. So, knot AND weave to produce a really secure thread end. Hint: Many beaders leave all weaving in of threads as a last step. This will ensure that you do not fill up a bead hole that may be needed during construction of the project.

Half Thread Method:

The Half Thread Method is based on two beading truths. One is that a short thread is easier to work with than a longer one. The other truth is that adding a new thread is tedious and laborious. With the Half Thread Method, you cut a thread that is twice as long so you eliminate the need to add thread. And, by using one half at a time, it is easier to work with than a longer thread. Begin by putting a stop bead in the middle of thread. You will be beading from the middle of the beadwork toward one end. Continue until instructed to stop. Then, remove the stop bead, put a needle on that thread end and continue beading from the middle of the beadwork to the other end.

Tip: The long tail thread can be troublesome for some beaders. To alleviate this problem, simply take a sticky note and loosely wrap the thread around it. Now take another sticky note and press it together with the first. This will make that long thread easy to handle while you are working with the needle thread. When you are ready to use the tail thread, open the sticky notes and un-wrap the thread.

Fitting to the Ball:

The glass balls for ornaments are not calibrated and there is variation in the size of seed beads even though they are all "size 11" and in bugle beads. The top portion of the ornament for Fire Flowers, Tropical Blues, Snow Pearl and Spring Wine, assumes the fringed band is in the middle of the ornament or below. If the beads you used fit on the ornament higher, then reduce the bead count on the top portion to 3 (same as in instructions) then 4 (instructions call for 5) and 4 (instructions call for 6). This will shorten the top section and fit better. You can also try using a different ornament ball.

Adding new thread:

1. End the old thread stitching down through the next column.
2. Cut a new thread and put a needle on it.
3. With the new thread, Stitch up through the previous column and down through the current column. Leave a tail of approximately 6 inches.
4. Take the new tail and old needle threads and tie a square knot.
5. Continue adding the fringe with the new needle. After a few new fringes are done, take the ends from the knot (both old needle and new tail threads), weave in and cut.

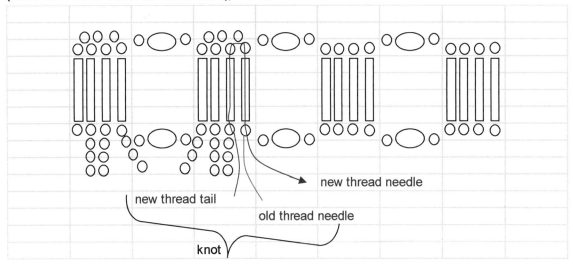

new thread needle

new thread tail

old thread needle

knot

Printed in Great Britain
by Amazon